The Beginning of Sorrows

EDWARD FOSTER

THE BEGINNING OF SORROWS

Marsh Hawk Press
East Rockaway, New York
2009

09 10 11 7 6 5 4 3 2 1 FIRST EDITION

Several poems and photographs included here were initially published in a chap-book entitled *A History of the Common Scale* (Texture Press, 2008). The author wishes to express his gratitude to Susan Smith Nash, founding editor of Texture Press, for her generosity and kindness and for her support of his work.

Marsh Hawk Press books are published by Poetry Mailing List, Inc., a not-for-profit corporation under section 501(c)3 United States Internal Revenue Code. Printed in the United States of America.

Text and titles: Plantin

Library of Congress Cataloging-in-Publication Data

Foster, Edward Halsey.
The beginning of sorrows / Edward Foster. -- 1st ed.
p. cm.
Includes bibliographical references.
ISBN-13: 978-0-9785555-9-7 (pbk.)
ISBN-10: 0-9785555-9-7 (pbk.)
I. Title.

PS3556.O7592B44 2009
811'.54--dc22

2009024017

Marsh Hawk Press
P.O. Box 206
East Rockaway, New York 11518-0206
www.marshhawkpress.org

CONTENTS

Photographs: p. 2: Western Massachusetts; p. 4: Covent Garden; p. 10: Greenfield, Mass.; p. 13: graveyard, New Hampshire; p. 17: Greenfield; p. 19: Greenfield; p. 25: Victorian study; p. 29: Greenfield; p. 32: Greenfield; p. 37: the Nile; p. 41: travel agency, Moscow; p. 46: Istanbul; p. 49: American boy; p. 50: Turkish boy; p. 54: Greenfield; p. 58: Ankara; p. 63: Miami; p. 67: Motel, New York State; p. 70: Ankara; p. 74: Uludağ, Turkey; p. 77: Mt. Monadnock; p. 80: Greenfield; p. 84: Greenfield; p. 87: Greenfield; p. 93: Afyan, Turkey; p. 97: water garden; p. 100: Galata Tower, Istanbul; p. 103: Tivoli, Italy.

The Beginning of Sorrows

"All sin consists in self-love and what is implied in this."
—Samuel Hopkins, *An Inquiry into the Nature of True Holiness* (1773)

"[T]wo cities have been formed by two loves: the earthly by the love of self, even to the contempt of God; the heavenly by the love of God, even to the contempt of self."
—St. Augustine, *The City of God* (early 5th cent.), trans. Marcus Dodds, D.D.

"[T]here is no level of human moral or social achievement in which there is not some corruption of inordinate self-love."
—Reinhold Niebuhr, *The Children of Light and the Children of Darkness* (1944)

Babes in the Woods

Let me understand
    these few things that we share.
I've come so far in writing down this lineage
I think we ought to rest and talk about the map.
I don't think, A., we should have turned left
down beyond the pasture. I know you were
convinced, having dreamed along the way,
but, darling, gender's not enough. I know
you like the lights of cities and believe
your insights can suffice, but that's got nothing
now to do with where we are. We're lost,
my dear; your propositions weren't enough.
You claimed you had a better route for us to share.
See the ruins we have passed.
You didn't know; you guessed.
It's time, my dear, we find our routes alone.

August

Not theatrical, casting another self in a leading role. — The parts
   have been played, and summer ends.

Don't stand so close or I'll imagine you were once my friend.

You did not call, yet you could see the clock. You waited, C., and

so did I. — I did not see your face, and now we leave the beach.
   The summer's gone, or almost gone,

and look: we're going to have a gathering, and all your family's
   coming home.

A Problem with Poems

"Ut pictura poesis." —Horace

I thought I would tell the truth, so how:
I would violate rules of civilized knowing and say what I see.
I would study my look, examine the mirror for stains.
I would rub none away.

I remember a woman in France who can't see
(a friend who knows nothing of men, what they most are).
She has all of the words but never has looked into her face or at mine.
She has never fingered this glass.
I will tell her just what I see.

Sloth

for Mustafa Ziyalan

Jonathan didn't rake his lawn the autumn he completed his experiment in seeing. The neighbors were angry with him when windstorms swept his leaves onto their property. Yet in this town people didn't complain openly about each other; it was considered unneighborly and rude.

It was such a quiet town! He had no desire to change anything in it. The silence in which his life seemed to float was what he wanted.

He spend his days indoors except for trips to the post office, the bank, and the supermarket. The checks from his family trust arrived each Monday, and on Tuesdays they were deposited. Thursdays he went shopping. Otherwise, he was at home, almost always alone and glad to be so.

Jonathan liked to think of himself as a spiritual man, but the religion he had cobbled together from texts in Plato and Thoreau would have made little sense to any but himself.

Many years earlier, Jonathan had been drawn to Plato's philosophy, in which notions of the ideal — ideal justice, ideal beauty, ideal goodness — intrigued him. Things and acts in the world, according to this theory, were striving to become ideal, to become a beautiful object, a beautiful thing, a beautiful self. Paradise, Jonathan concluded, was ultimate resolution, stillness and calm.

He had sought that calm first by trying to slow all of his feelings and actions. He walked slowly and methodically. He ate his food slowly. He lay in bed until noon and went back to bed after dinner. And most important, or so he said, he learned to meditate. For a short while, this had felt tedious, but only for a short while.

In *Walden*, he had read, "Things do not change; we change. Sell your clothes and keep your thoughts. God will see that you do not want society." Here, Jonathan believed, was the key to immortality: change led to death, so if one would live forever, one must focus on static "things" and "thoughts," and avoid society, where rules and behavior were continually evolving.

Jonathan concluded that if he were to live forever, nothing should change. It was his "obligation" or "duty" to be sure things remained as they were. He must be mindful and attentive and do nothing that would alter the world.

He preserved objects. He kept copies of the town newspaper (which he rarely read), old bank statements and the envelopes in which his checks arrived, used cans and plastic food containers, clothes he did not intend to wear again, old appliances, dishes, pans, and so forth.

Everything he preserved was treated with respect.

Aside from his weekly round in the world at large (post office, bank, supermarket), there was little in his life except his objects. They were enough.

Sex was extraneous. He had never had much interest in girls and no interest in boys. Most girls appeared to be looking for a husband with ambitions, but Jonathan singled out the few in town who were too lazy or unambitious themselves to want more than attention.

Among these, the one who satisfied him most was Brenda, and she was one of very few people he brought to his house. He believed that she suffered from some as yet unidentified disease. He would test her from time to time by leaving her in one room and saying he would be back in a while. If "a while" were an hour or more, she would still be there when he returned. He got from this much the same pleasure that he derived from meditation: the sense that he was now in contact with essence, things as they are.

With time, Brenda became Jonathan's notion of perfection, unfazed by feeling or thought. He would sit across from her and take pleasure in studying her passivity. She was as motionless as a mannequin. Eventually Jonathan realized that he could have all that Brenda offered him without having the person herself. Memory was all he needed.

Jonathan found he could achieve Zen-like clarity and calm whenever he looked at objects. He could sit for many hours, watching. He would forget what the object was and would enter into a deeply peaceful state in which time did not seem to exist.

He would not have called himself lazy. What he was doing was purposeful. It was a spiritual life, and, to his way of thinking, far more meaningful that anything else a person might feel he needed.

There was a brief period during which the local priest would visit Jonathan. The priest tried to change his ways. The priest spoke about "God's world" and the need to have a "vocation," but the priest, said Jonathan, was wrong. Objects exist for their own sake. They have nothing to do with God. They are simply there. "You must accept this," he told the priest.

And Jonathan was happy. His life excluded everything unpleasant. He had little to do outside his weekly chores, and when they were done, he could begin his meditations again.

The leaves, blowing around the yard, swept onto the neighbor's lawn. But he could not find words for what he saw. He focused on the leaves and watched them in his mind.

Not to Be Trusted

In that dream, I didn't ask her out.
That part's known and always true.
Anyone who'd take a look would know.
It's spring.

The girls across the street
have yellow tulips coming up
And tolerate my messy yard.

None of us have children making noise.
So that's a plus, the girls would say.
But we stay far apart.
So really:
        who made up the rumor?

This poem can't tell all the truth (you know why)
re: what we did. It simply tells us
what we felt and seem.
The deeper facts we closet with ourselves.

The Lady Did Not Hear

"Inner voice"?
            Listen, lady,
the you with whom I talk must be real.
To speak, I must create you every day
and hear your lessons like a boy.
I say: I'm famished for your touch.

My landscape has a golden swan, a savior,
ladies like yourself with capes and parasols.
Gently, lady speaks to me
in tones that make it sound
as if this savior comes
to make all wonder.

So it's Lohengrin (inside his secret life),
transfigured as a swan.
That's the part you never see.

The swan is cruel, or could be cruel,
bringing to the rhythm of the work
its end. And nothing of this could be seen
by those like you with no tradition left.

Not in her.
No final talk
about the failures
we exchange.

Greed

Brenda wanted everything for herself. She cultivated an ability not to respond emotionally to anything anyone said or did. As a child, she was considered autistic and was given special help at school. She was not autistic, however, and the authorities eventually realized that her problem lay in another direction for which they had no name.

The "problem" began when Brenda was three. Her father told her that she must share her toys with her baby brother. She started to cry, so he slapped her and sent her to her room.

As she lay there in bed, she decided that her toys would always be hers, and she began teaching herself to imagine each — the doll, the building blocks, the make-up kit — so well that its image in her mind was stronger than the object itself. She could sit quietly in a chair and envision the building blocks, for example, and build a fantasy bridge that was bigger than herself. In her fantasy she could walk across and under the bridge. She could feel its textures and temperature, and when she tired of it, she could take it apart and put the pieces back in their imaginary box. All this time, she was perfectly still.

Brenda spent so much time sitting and imagining that her face eventually lost all of its natural expression. She refused to exercise, and when the children in her class went outdoors for recess, she remained at her desk imaging her possessions. The teachers soon abandoned any attempt to convince her to join the other children. Everyone ignored Brenda insofar as they could. For a while, they had made fun of her, but as she never responded to their taunts and sat passively, eventually everyone left her to her own devices.

The same was true at home. Her mother would bring food to Brenda's room, but Brenda never ate when anyone was around. Her mother would find the dishes empty and Brenda sitting as if she had not moved in the interim.

As she grew older, she had no interest in sex — even with the young man, Jonathan, who would call from time to time and ask her to come over to his house to visit.

[14]

She liked to visit him because he was so undemanding. He would ask her to sit in his living room, and after a few pleasantries, he would leave her, and this gave her an opportunity to enter him into her world of imagined objects.

Eventually Jonathan stopped inviting her to his house, and that was fine with her. She possessed all of him that she needed, and none of it was threatening. She could put the pieces of him together and take them apart, and this gave great pleasure that she would never have to admit to anyone.

There was a new religious group in the town. They gathered each evening to meditate in hopes of reaching what their leader called "the highest reality." The leader — a young man who had spent much of his adult life looking for spiritual enlightenment in the Himalayas — said that this reality involved perfect stasis. He claimed that when this point was reached, desire no longer existed because one had "everything."

Brenda was known for her trance-like silence, and the leader, hearing this, visited her and proclaimed to his followers that Brenda had reached "the highest reality." Since she neither affirmed nor denied this, the leader went on to say that in her perfection there was no need even to reason; she had all that was needed: she had transcended externality and had embarked on the truly divine.

From then on, the leader and his followers would periodically visit Brenda, who, not moving, would receive them with perfect calm. But that "calm," of course, was simply the mask behind which Brenda could observe each of her devotees and record in her brain those elements that distinguished him or her from others and the rest of the objects that comprised the totality of her desired world.

Being Baseless

The list of judges giving cash says no hope here, and so no hope
    will be. We're baseless,
but I'd like your voice to speak, tho gathering from those few
    communications you send now,
our conversation's reached its end. So, let's release the polish and
    the light;
they've done their work and, look, we've all moved back to one more
steady state. We're playing Odd Man Out again, tho had I had my
    choice, today we'd watch those old
cartoons about the bearded man and how the woman who's name
    I can't recall
ran away. Your stuff.

That was the stuff of childhood, and you chased her skirt because
    art's just a map for life with overtones,
or so you said. But, look, there really was a better figuration in the
    work,
way deep behind the image so that our eyes created new born plea-
    sure, but then you had your wife
and I had mine, and that was that. We kept ourselves at home,
    entertaining guests. Nothing should have
held us back, but we made life and language flat and were discreet.

Hanging On

All around, the walls that line
our city start to break.
The deadly things pass through.
We have no children left.
There's no concern for who comes first,
just us and all this poisoned air we drink
to hold us down as we hold it.

These walls, we know, will all come down.
The forces whom we saw so eager at the gate
have come to end our struggle
in their name.

We see them line themselves along the road.
They say we mustn't say we disapprove
or want to stay. We're not allowed to say
our time is not yet done.

Why should we care?
We know
that everything must end.

Let poison reach us through these walls.
Be calm, let each of us be calm.
Take punishment
as if we'd really want
the forces at the gate
to be as honored
as history
must say they were.

Tapping the Moon

Waxed strangely —
I never liked this moon
or any moon. I'm tired of her lectures
on the evil passing through the world.
                    Elves, fairies, wolves,
I'd embrace them all, these lunar creatures
before I'd take one Lady Moon like her,
                    passing through my soul.
Out there as mid-day passes by, those who were my friends
pursue their fame. I'm strangely home.

J. in the Snow

But we did:
we did just what you said,
or what we thought you'd say,
if you would speak it.

And did the humble thing,
and felt as if, here,
at last,
the thing were done.

But you recoiled
into your paternal self,
your world,
tho you denied
complicity with it.

But J., there's no one
here believing now.

Just look: this February day
is chilly, and the snow
keeps coming down.

All things around reduce
themselves to sycophant delight:
the children playing in the snow,
they'll be yours now.

The fault lines
cut between each son,
and then erupt to
bring calm back again.

His Sons Grow Old

[*Sultan Murad III had twenty potential heirs. Ottoman custom required that all but one should die immediately after their father. Of the nineteen thus killed, one was a child found by the executioner eating chestnuts. The boy begged that he be spared until the chestnuts were gone, but the executioner, knowing his obligation, wrapped a silk handkerchief around the boy's neck and strangled him.*]

The old man
never cared
for me or them.

Determined sons are best.
— stolen from the cradle,
weaklings,
trained by overbearing women,
thrust upon dark stages,
forced to sing softly
to mothers and ambitious girls.
No modern tedium
could lend us more.

How else to better time,
reduce its cavern past to
confidence? Look: those people
could be heroes, thinking they
could give us all they never got:
Worship! Paradise! Eternity!

No, sweet prince,
like you, your sons grow old
before their time.

Her Body of Law

Where do you write it down when the lady smiles again, this day of rain? The rain, raining down on her who has not you but all men who line the shore, men whose gods release bouquets of iris on her self. She is the one that my, and your, young men pursue. She knows we won't, and so she beckons us to join her in the gardens that line her island distant from the farther shore.

Our anger at all we've heard won't stop. "Be calm," she says. "They're never cruel for long."

And when she leaves, her entourage is gone as well. So you and I are left to wonder what has given her so much. The waters rise and reach our lips. We drink and all goes dark.

The lady knows the secret to survive. "Have you ever seen a young man die?" she asked me once. "Do you know the struggle I prepare for each?"

Of course. I've seen her do it, and I understand why you and I, and all like-minded men, must never leave this lake, this island, or could elsewhere feel at least the warmth within the rain coming down.

Poets, Set Your Watches: The Death of Ilhan Berk

Slender stalk — a field I'd enter, trespass —
But where did Alice go? She was known to touch us all,
angelic, as I think we said, angelic — the only one to criticize each
    of us
for his fault and have no fault her own. Even then the century was
    shutting down.
As for now, I place a row of stones upon her stone,
mystical design that can mean nothing anymore.
It used to hold a secret, a cabalistic tone —
an engine of the universe that horribly would groan and clack
until she set our time — but time itself shuts down these doings, too.

And holding hands, we'd penetrate so deep within the field
we scared ourselves, thinking we would never see our friends again.
Among the slender stalks, each stalk, sweet surface,
held a scent we'd feed ourselves, knowing rapture.
These were secrets then, and poets dressed for Carnival.
The stalks grew old. They made disease. We could be happy
if we had not thought the field we counted real
held things that keep.

This Time Left Behind (All of the Above)

You have done it to yourself, all of it —
How else would winter friends lie now?

Watch this passing one gather up his shawl
and wrap himself so well,
he disappears beneath the cloth.

Just one small part remains (memory aside),
enough to say
that he would lie here once.

And now that particle is in a box.
We place it on the highest shelf,
where all is dark,
almost out of reach.

This remains the spot where former friends are kept —
along with sons too sharp to wait.
All those who once were here, with whom he'd play,
right there, down on beds of flowers, far below.

This was
a lovely spot.
Together he and others
made it so.

From time to time, we take the boxes down
and look inside.
So many do we find who still can
breathe and speak enough to live!
Dear friends, it is enough to make us laugh.
It tickles us, and turns life upside down
as you would do the same with me.

And as with babies (we had none) just beginning, so.
We had to choose this way of doing things
so all of us could live. And so the boxes
give a record of our common past.
It isn't nice you know and wasn't meant to be.

Was He Ever There?

"*Erōs* is, with only a few exceptions, utterly one-sided. You can be longed for, loved (*philein*), desired 'in return' (*anti-*) with no problems, but for the Greeks there can be no mutual   *erōs*, not concurrently." —James Davidson, *The Greeks and Greek Love*

The imagined one, the one above the
roof, my patriarch of skies. We see him
pointing out from posters.
We count the chains that twist about his neck.

Who captured him?
Who pushed aside the girl
yet still brought lethargy?
Our breath is made of his.
We satiate his need.
We pleasure him.

Seeding the Sky

No Kalypso,
no lustrous lady,
no loom,
no harvest.

No reason, historical cause,
causality, out of itself
as if that had been. In the sky,
the men of the sky,
seeding the earth in the way
the great gods used to do.

The folks down there
listen to rain,
but don't understand,
trapping their minds
in closets, cabinets, boxes.

So they were taught, and how
much I wanted to join
you never can know.

To possess and belong,
protecting the rights
that used to accrue.
But that's all
shut down. The engine
is gone, kerplunk.

All of it gone
except the usual rain.

The Centerfold My Friend Would Be

"He was entrancing, with that epicene beauty which in extreme youth
sings aloud for love and withers at the first cold wind."
—Evelyn Waugh, *Brideshead Revisited: The Sacred and Profane
Memories of Captain Charles Ryder* (1945)

What's here to ask, farmer boy? you say, and being mean, I ask as
    much of you.
And so, my paper friend, I ask aloud, What reason do you have to
    stay?
The reason you say you and your art's only art, is (why?).
Now could you be as much as what I see? (You like to laugh.)
Could you be as relished as the movement that I see, looking out
    and into crowds,
and there you like a boy wearing just those jeans I like and so touch
    me (as I touch you).
You're really fresh, a farmer's boy, plucked clean. And do you know
    because I sew
seeds deep for you within your heart, and mine? Why is it only you
    (or part of you)
this poem wants to touch as you touch me when I'm exactly you?
And why am I so lucky meeting you right down here on your end-
    lessly imagined farm?

Portia's Complaint

I.

Looking through the window
at the boys walking home,
she magically could call the daylight
back, remembered climes and sound.
It's winter now. (I know her mind.)
Feel this: the icicles that will not
melt. Remember then this time.
Lay your fingers on her chair. She
cannot age. In this, she cannot be.
That icicle divides the boys
from that old time when some
believed she had the right to rule.

Try to touch her through the icy glass.
Remember time. Break in and
run your fingers in her frost.
One winter's day, you had a
friend, not her (her role was then
to teach). You ask for warmth.
Go back: decide. Hear the stories
made for ears that now
no longer hear.

II.

Think only sound. Don't look outside
the frost or glass today. Only hear.
In her snow, the children have their day.
You would not hurt. They freeze,

made into ice. Hear their icy fingers
crack. Close your eyes, imagining
their heads now make the sound of glass.
Remember time. Hear them shout, and let
that part be in your mind. The dogs can't
bark, and icicles reclaim the world.
The mothers search and cannot find.

The fathers search and cannot find.
The family is a thing we all forget.
And then we know the word
because of sound. We do not see.

The children cannot slide along
the snow. Listen to the fingers
crack. The cracking only
says you can.

III.

I cannot reason what she wants.
As if to hear it said would make it care.
We grant that she is clever and denotes
herself as capable and kind. We recall
her sitting in a lounge chair late in June,
waiting for the sound. She was a fascination
to her child. Her husband liked her, too.
Now she feels herself along, waiting
for the time. But what will matter if
it's not the thing she was?

Smiles never tell you what you need
to know. We come to her because of
ease, the way our shoulders languish

next to hers. Since people didn't seem
to come again, or want to come,
she manufactured how she felt, with toys.

IV.

This one thought clothes make the man.
Just one day the mirror showed
him what he was and liked. Looking out
the window all he saw was overcast.

He watched the animals outside his bedroom.
In his mind, he ran across the snow
like squirrels and cats he saw.
Squirrels, he knew, can tell what's
deeply underneath the snow.

Just one day he saw him, too, the way he was.
The sky was overcast. No one saw,
guessing what he saw. He saw the dark, black
snow, but in his mind, he looked into the mirror
and found the parts to hide.

Thus the world was right:
clothes really make the man.

V.

Trying to be solemn, to elevate the
self into a Christian mind,
where each one counts, and,
knowing just the same, "respects"
the selves of others. What a
dream! How to be a sparrow in the

snow! — the snow as white as every
church he'd ever known. Conflict over all:
Armageddon as an angry name. How good
it might have been to be the goodly man,
the father of us all.

How good it might have been to be
the one his child might want.
    Or so he saw.

As for the child himself,
he's doing fine.

Envy

Within this house I've gathered what I need. I've haunted auctions, antique stores, and stores online, looking for the furnishings that express my nature. Everything must be the way it should and what I want, and I treat the things I gather with respect. If there's anything I need, I buy and make it mine. This house out on its spit of land makes me feel as if my home were sailing out to unknown seas, like something in a book for boys. And that, to me, is what I want and what, times past, others did.

Perfection means owning what your cultivated taste insists you need. That's the way it used to be for everyone who'd mastered elements that made our culture work. Then came the change, and people failed to dress in ways we'd all agreed were elegant and fine. Instead they dressed in violation of what the culture then comprised, and so the culture changed itself or seemed to change, tho underneath the surface, all those gears, belts, chains are what they ever were.

Here's my report: the trouble with this world began the day men gave up wearing uniforms and polishing their boots a slicker hue, things you and I have never failed to do ourselves, but doing which has meant one thing: that we're alone, the last ones of the breed, and people don't agree with what we like and, therefore, never really see us on the street (or else they think us odd). But we see them, and there's the rub, for kindness never corresponds to what you feel in any case. Kindness is a fiction; the world is cold, and all that generates our greatest heat is need. You and I are like things people trip against and never see. That gives us force. For we possess their spirit in the end, know them better than they know themselves, and need never give that insight back.

We own the world we see and feel our pathos for the residents who think that it's enough simply buying what their neighbors buy or using chemicals to cure their aging bodies so at seventy they think they feel the way they did at twenty-five. They've lost all touch with need, the way things really are, for need is not performance or an act and will not age. It means: possess and be. It means we need to run soft hands across the polish on well made cabinets, armoires, and cotton jeans. Need means possess, and not possess the way a banker does but rather own the feel itself, the elements of grace and dance that constitute the very seed of truth. That's what being human is.

And so I lock myself and you inside and dress ourselves, the mirror serving well, in clothes that comfort skin. I sit here on the hassock watching our reflections talking back about the evening and tremors in the air. This means: to own. This means: to take the flavor out of air, condense it like a rose, and feel totalities of what we want: perfection.

The other day a girl in jeans walked past me on the street. She would not see anything but her destination, yet in my mind I ran my fingers on her shirt. She never knew. I took her for my own and brought her home. I sat her on this hassock and studied how her hair swept back and how she wore her flesh, all of which in other worlds would be obscene.

But not in mine and yours. That's the magic that we understand, you and I: how things change according to our needs. Look again along the contours fitting to that girl. Embrace her ankles, own her, dress her as you will. I make those ankles mine. The meaning's only this: to need. No passion, no desire: those are very different (chilly) things. Not love, of course, or other states of mind we make to hide the deepest self: the need. There's nothing dirty in creating what we need. At that point, we cannot be wrong. Perfection is the only termination we allow our joy.

If culture's to survive, changes must be made. Complexities of feeling that end in emptiness must go. Think of Tristan, Romeo, and other figures who were false to feelings deep within themselves and who were made to think that satisfaction lay with owning others, and being owned. How did their efforts end?

There's just one way all acts conclude, and that is solitary death. Avoid the lies of lovers. Cultivate need: call it yours, call it mine, and I am you. That's how this selfish culture works, or should. Construct a home from what you've learned of taste. Cultivate your jealousies and discontent and make your home be nothing more or less than what you are.

[39]

Melting Snow

Spring is sharp wind and melting snow (the children said).
Living in the country, almost new, where you and those like you
    most likely won't be seen.

New neighbors stopping by would shake my hand. Examining my
    hair and pictures on the wall,
they satisfy themselves that nothing here whatever satisfies their
    need.

Oh, well: more expectations never met, any spring. Nothing
    answers, and in keeping,
I respond when they are gone: It's spring! At last the snow is almost
    gone.

At least we know what neighbors want. Another year is here.
I like these people. They are my real. They are my melting snow.

The Falcon

(1)

The dream's enamel, rainbow blue,
within a shadow's
boyish glow.

Begging, I, this once my needs be met,
the beach boy (or his image, you would say),
throwing me a ball beneath a Carribean sun,
was never (in your version) there,
whatever else I felt.

If so, I wouldn't mind:
seeing him was all I'd need.

Aside from dreams,
he lives, for me, in magazines,
and that's enough.

He's like a falcon,
and I can't escape his satisfaction.

(2)

The French priest in another dream
improved our looks, grew younger,
seducing each of us who watched.

Everything again was rainbow blue.

In this solemn rite, he clarified the meaning
left to men like me and you,
holding tight.

I felt as if his
were a private church,
blue with ikons which we'd made ourselves

and which I took for images of truth,
until that falcon found me out.

Your Somewhat Symbolic Mind

1.

Last night's fiction
recited with silk and reddened
lips, to please,
about the man who
gardened, spent his life
cultivating things his children
might enjoy. Flowers
blossomed everywhere.

The kindness in the children,
as he wished,
was clear, transparent.
He watched their anger grow.

He owned himself out of fear.
But as a friend
his friends had found him ghostly,
clothed in colors only
victims understood.

His walls were thin.
Car doors would slam.

People hurried by.
Now no one looks.

His secrecy is fragile after all.

He never banked on that.

2.

He'd say,
I have to know you well
before I speak.

The air around his place
is dry.

And now
there's nothing still
within the branches
in his garden
but the air.

Wrath

Her mother took her to meet the town Santa Claus, who rode around on a fire truck, stopping wherever children gathered in front of their homes and waved. They could sit on his lap and tell him what they wanted for Christmas, and when it was her turn, she told him she wanted a fire truck like his. She was five years old and didn't know the truck belonged to the town, but she loved what she saw and, in the way children do, imagined what she might make of it, perhaps live in it with her toys and her mother and father. She would not let her brother live there; he would stay in the house. He was seven and kind to her only when her parents were around. At dinner earlier that week when her father left the table to answer the phone and her mother was in the kitchen, her brother had pushed her plate onto the floor, and she had been beaten because he had said she was angry at something he'd said just to tease her and had pushed the plate on purpose.

This was in 1957.

That Christmas her mother gave her a toy fire truck and said that it was from Santa and that he would give her a big one when she was older. She was disappointed that this truck was small, but she believed her mother and thought that it was the promise of better things to come. Her brother, however, said that only boys had fire trucks and that she should give it to him. She refused and hid it in her closet, for she feared her brother and did not want him to find it. But while she was asleep, he did find it and in the quiet night took it to the driveway and set it near the rear wheels of his father's car. The next morning, when his father left for work, he did not see the fire truck and, as expected, rolled the car over it as he backed down the driveway, and the truck was crushed.

Children do such things all the time, of course, and in part, it may be, these cruelties help to make us what we are. For example, many of us find ourselves in middle management positions, and although we are nothing special and are easily replaced, we begin to think of people under us in terms of dollars and cents. If we have to fire them, we think of it as simply part of the job and feel no guilt but rather feel such pleasure as her brother felt when the fire truck was destroyed, and no one could blame him for it. His mother had berated her for being so careless as to leave her new toy in the driveway, and no one believed her when she said she had left it in her closet. It is secret pleasures that we most enjoy.

But these have repercussions, and she grew up with that fire truck unchanging in her mind as if wrapped like a chrysalis. The truck was the one great thing in her childhood that she felt she had wanted and been denied, and now it was too late. In symbolic form the truck told her something strange and irrational about the nature of the world and how she must respond. It was as if whatever might quench the fires of anger in her soul were no longer there. Revenge grew within her spirit until she began to see enemies everywhere and needed to corral them to make them safe. She trained herself to be efficient and, to all appearances, faultless in manners and in dress, and so she impressed her employers, for they knew that whatever they asked her to do, she would do it well. She pretended to be shy but accommodated their needs and slept with them, women as well as men, and laughed at their humor but worked very hard.

We would see her in the halls talking to one of the men (or women) from upstairs, and they would be bending over her as if she were a child, but there was no mistaking the desire in their gestures and their smiles. Eventually she got exactly what she felt she had to have, which was the directorship of human resources, which meant that it was her job not only to find workers for openings in our business but also to keep the records that show how well or poorly people do their jobs.

She is most efficient and can with ease inform a long-term employee that he is not needed anymore. If you do not cross her and do your job as efficiently as she does hers, you do survive.

Poetic Diction

No grammar worth dreaming,
   no lies built up from clauses,
all of it plain, and, Leo, why did you ask,
   all of a sudden,
    now that we're here in a room
where, mostly, as well you may know,
   people choose to be alone?

Meanwhile, delegate manners,
   let me know how you wish me
to act and dress.

Shall I polish
   my manners and style?

That seems a concern.

Exactly which suit
   would you like me
   to wear?

Whatever you ask, I'll happily give.
   I'll scratch you and fawn.
I'll examine your poems
   and provide them with praise.

American boy

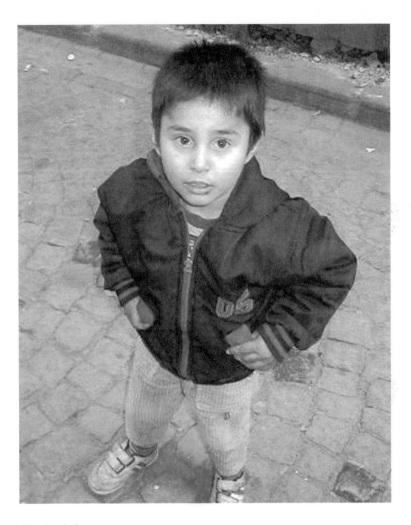

Turkish boy

Capt. Bligh in Academe

I think again,
    as I have thought,
        for moons and moons,

about the jolly man
    with office space.

He's no true scholar,
    tho he'd have us
        think he is,

but let us say this much:
    he knows his facts

although he can't coordinate
    such things
        beyond a flimsy line.

He's now become an academic god,
    with titles, and much feared
        (as he would like to hear us say),

calling to account
    all who do not do
        exactly as he says.

For those of us who listen close,
    he has a message
        he's been promising to tell,

something that he says
    will let us know
        his quality of mind.

I settle in
　　and bend my ear
　　　　beneath his lips.

I cannot hear his snore,

and yet I know
　　our leader
　　　　is asleep.

Don't Ask

The army said don't tell. I told.
I told them what I'd seen last night in clubs
they never knew about.

I told them why I failed to vote and how.

I told them that my mother had grown old.
The doctors said that operations do her good.
She died. I told the army that.

I told the army that I'd like to serve in Vietnam
now that fighting's stopped
and Saigon is a world resort.

I told them truths I wouldn't tell my friends.
I lay my issues bare.

I begged them to respond.
As always in this democratic land,
they serve no answers yet.

The Model That You Thought Was Almost You

is just a foxman in his lair.
Watch him flash his look,
and lounge in his café
as if we'd be in Paris, too,
to wander up the hill to Montparnasse
or look for contacts
dressed like him.

No one wants me there, for sure,
but here's my secret: no one wants you either,
Juan, (there at least),
and this you know.
Look like him
and find you're
just another fish,
respected there
in elegant attire,
resurrected for an ad
in magazines
read by certain men.

Like me!

Look close: your jacket's
soft as silk. Mine's not.
Your outfit must have
cost a bundle.

Implied Conclusion

How does the self critique the self? What is meant by
evidence within? Who speaks this evening, R.?

Not you.

We took a vote.
We decided that
tonight you won't be heard.

We just won't
listen to your words.

And then we said
your history's a fiction.

Disliking you,
we feel
that our decisions
must suffice.

Basic Thought

No confection to be had: nothing to recall.
All women then would offer. We learn.
I'm on my guard. However much you want,
I want it back. Interest counts. So it is
within my rooms, I keep things neat and clean,
as I was told.
                    As for books,
I simply don't have room.
I get enough of reason down at work, you say.
Just once, you pay the bills, and then for me
there's nothing left to do.

Gluttony
for Roy and Chris

Although bulimic and small, Catherine was rapacious in her need for control. Her office was furnished with an immense desk and the largest monitor she could find. She packed her own lunch, and everyday it sat beside her keyboard until noon, a tub of yoghurt and a small container of diet ice cream. She ate as little as she felt she safely could and trained herself to think of other things.

All of the artists gave her obeisance and they had to. They fed her out of their own self-esteem, admitting that they could not have survived without her. Whatever they achieved had to be seen, in part, as the result of her efforts. They could not celebrate the sale of a painting or a favorable review without giving her credit. Management, as she understood it, did not merely manage; it made things possible.

Catherine needed to see every artist in the studio complex often. Beside her desk she had chairs on which they could sit. She did not like them to stand. The chairs were somewhat lower than her own, and the artists felt like children as they talked to her. She would judge them all the time.

Catherine held herself high. She believed that the artists in the complex would not survive without her efforts. There was an older woman, Constanza, who made decorative vases from multi-colored clay. Out back were kilns. Catherine had raised money for the kilns and was thanked in Constanza's brochure promoting her work. An exhibit in Chelsea had been arranged by Catherine. Constanza was now quite famous, and Catherine knew that she herself was responsible for that. So did the critics who called her for information about Constanza rather than call Constanza herself. Catherine negotiated prices for Constanza's work, and Constanza thanked her.

Catherine's son, Absalom, graduated from a small college where he had majored in theology because his mother, who attended church regularly, had said he should, believing that he was fit to be a priest. But he was much too shy for such responsibilities, and so she made him her assistant, a job that did not require him to appear in public unless she said he must. She convinced her board of directors that Absalom was her right arm as it were, and they did not care as long as the complex made money. Absalom's principal jobs were cleaning the hallways late at night and keeping the books. When Catherine planned to say something unpleasant to one of the artists — as when she had to expel one for failing to pay his rent — she would tell Absalom to join her so that there would be a witness in case the artist grew angry and made trouble.

Absalom was without ambition. He had given that to her. She told him what he should do and why it should be done. She connected three of the studios in such a way that they formed an apartment for him. People who saw them together and did not know who they were thought that they must be lovers — a May/September romance — and were happy to see that. The young man was smitten, they thought, and, like all young men in such relationships, had little desire or ambition for himself. His one desire was to please his lover.

But it was not love. The peaceful Absalom had lost all desire for a companion as well as for that painful ambition that drives the rest of us to succeed. He had never had more than a glimmer of the inner lives of other people and their wants. He did as he was told and was content. Things seemed to be as they always had been. He had been consumed from childhood by his mother's needs.

Catherine had no ability as an artist nor did she feel a need for that. She had done her college thesis on Max Ernst and thought herself an expert on his style. Many years ago, she had collected essays on Ernst from experts. Most were college instructors or museum curators, and all were well known in their respective fields. They were more alert to fashions in the art world than she, and she knew that, but after all, it was she who made the book possible. She thought of them as stars in a constellation she had made herself.

Catherine wrote the introduction, depending wholly on the opinions of others, and contributed to the cost of publishing the book by a major house, where the editors were much interested in Ernst but were certain that this particular book would not sell enough to cover its

[61]

costs, as proved to be the case. Catherine bought half the print run and gave copies to visitors to the studio complex whom she wished to impress. They and the artists and everyone else knew that she was no expert on Ernst or anything in art. But she managed the complex well, and they learned to need her. In short, she had made herself essential to a world to which she did not belong.

Catherine did not realize that many people knew and talked about this. As management, she was protected from the beliefs of others; they would only tell her what they thought she wanted to hear. The artists needed her to do the work that otherwise might interfere with their own. They knew what Catherine had to consume, and so they gave her praise. In turn, she gave them security and a place to work.

What the artists did not realize, or did not want to admit, was that she drained them of more than they chose to give. When they most depended on her, as, for example, when sales were slow and they could not pay the full month's rent, she would ratchet up her demands for obeisance. She would say nothing directly, but they immediately understood that they must spend more time with her and talk about her contributions to art.

Medication

(1)

Watch out! She'll flail around
in words, accusing you and me of things
she brought about herself.

Now that you and I no longer
stand alone, she brings us issues
to debate.

How to judge a failure,
or her secret wish?

A child could do it;
why not we?

(2)

Bill's poems then got shorter.

Very sly, he said.
When you're old,
there's so much less to say.

He'd seen her work bursting into empty lines,
measured by her praising self.

It's best to leave the world, he said,
before your time has come.

Portia Hopes To Finish Last

Wrap it up, Portia. The blood will flow,
and doctors will predict
another end. The lucky know what's next.
You'll never satisfy yourself with sleep,
my dear. The terminus must like
the brash young moving (*moving*) in
until the room is full.
Outside silence, there's no life left.
You used to feel so good
to touch,
so much above it all, but as your
people start to leave, the others
turn from you.

Your Happiness or Mine?

We found him light — undisguised,
controlled, directed wholly by himself, yet
worshiped by his wife (how many men
could say as much?), chosen.

Why assent to any man like that?

Now that you and I have reached
a certain age, we can withdraw,
put on an act, and be reserved.

Yesterday the room would shrink
until my knees touched yours, so
now I wait politely, hoping
that he'll leave, and shut the door.

We Propose

We made proposals in
the delicate field
where sons and daughters
hesitate to go.

The reasons, as the elderly can tell,
must stay obscure:
My condition must be solitude,
just you and I.
Children must not come or call.

The older people
seem the greediest, yet sane:
protecting futures
by remaining as they
think they were.

You thought that coming here would be a joke:
but friendship's not a game, dear and deadly Dan,
nor should a child see how quickly it can pass.

The Man All Wet with Dew

I'll capture his full moon
that will not let me sleep.

Why affect his manner
if all we get is rest from hope?

Flying is good.
Falling is best.

Spring has come, and you are here.
Everything on time.
Kültür, Cacophony,
Birds.

Like the birds,
beware, my friend —
the spring and birth will end.

The flowers bloom,
but then we ask what's next.
Dry August,
when the angels start to sing.

Remember:
summer can't remember spring.
Flowers, too, will end.
The girls respond
in ways we won't maintain.
Love always goes away.

Spring I

Placid Spring with windows! —
Hey, we get to watch the birds.
The world will measure light again,
my clever aunt would say, if she
were still alive. No more springs for
her. She scattered seeds for robins.
I ought to be less cruel and close
the door to all such memories.
Allergies blossom with the plants.
A desert would be nice, inspiring
another gentleman's hormonal rage.
Close all the doors. Birds live
to wake us up. Last night I hardly slept.

Farewell to the Philosopher Who Could Not Do His Job

I know enough to know
most things that you design won't work.
The I you saw reflected
was not the one
that's leaving now.
The I you see would stick around
and argue.
Well, argue now as you shift gears
and merge with all the rest.
You said, you really said,
you wanted subtlety
and systematic thought
within: fulfillment —
more than what you'd
like to give.

Destruction of the Good

Down this short street all lawns were once a field.
You see the little homes where people share their meat.
The franchise on the corner gives an income to my cousin Will.

Years ago he was our nation's hero, a Navy Seal, a wonder to our land.
The rockers on his porch are made from pine trees shipped from
    Maine,
the closest he will come to how we lived.

I've watched him watch our land grow old.
We rarely spoke.

There wasn't time for him, or memories of his battleship.
We sat and sit and wait.
The world right now is not the one he made.

The Personal Is Political

He reasserts his mission. They flock back in.
He feeds them, makes them reach.
He learns from them another language of deceit.
He watches them, hard for cash,
     reconstruct what others tore apart.
I think his secret word's "revenge."

But as for us
(can I assume I speak for you?),
we hold the door,
nor do we think
to give an opening to grace.

We watch his face, and grin.
(no buzzard has to fear, because
he will be back, and
simply feeling cold, pursues,
as if no human could restrain
his look.) It's all too much,
and yet this ever vapid round
consoles.

The People Making Money for You

Others never need to think about such things as much.

Ugliness in mirrors keeps them down.

They strengthen our economy.

And all have dogs —
big ones in many colors,
sometimes plaid.

These people eat their food in little gulps.

These people tell us what they'll do when they get old.

New Buildings in Istanbul

I wouldn't have thought the dreams
    would languish, I so seldom heard
them wake. It's hard to know just what
    they'd say or why. They disappeared
so fast. There was the one about the train
    in Istanbul, new ways to get around
that place, where friends no longer speak
    to me, lounging in the district,
where no one wants to be.

I fear them. They disrupt, or could disrupt,
    this life and ours. They have no recourse
now that business buildings march on down
    to mosques like spacemen in a movie
dream. Now you can't dream the way
    you did. I take you, boy, as always
in your jeans. I want to see, but all these buildings
    and their boys seem so much older than
they are. We want a newer crop, as these
    wear suits and carry guns.
Oh, second self, I do not fear
    their lie.

Empaneled in Jersey City

What is the proper learning, the choice
to take up this or that, not to get in someone's way
or interfere with someone's view? We want to know
enough to leave the details out.

Too many times the case was tried.
We gave our evidence, telling judges just what
we thought we knew. Disputes arose.
The jury left and thought about the case,
then asked for testimony from friends who
told them dreams, everything they'd think was right.

Those formulas had all been tried. Their flaws we once
had pointed out. And judges left to join their families
on foreign ground, leaving us to wait for further trials.
Our friends ran out, scot free.
Whose democracy was that?

Living in the Modern World

It's cold out there
and so I traveled
to the Hello Inn.

I warmed my hands
beside the roaring blaze
and had a drink.

    But

they charge too much for rooms,
the food is never cheap.
And people rarely talk to you
(aside from colleagues stopping by
to see if you agree with this or that).

    And

The Hello Inn
(Like others in that chain)
offers nothing to enlighten,
no metaphysics,
nothing that helps explain.

    But

The boy who runs the desk
has all the questions and the answers
memorized.

    If

you stick to the script,
no matter what you ask,
he politely gives you the answers you wish.

And so

I ask.

The Floozy Eating Your Soup

Child porno extras get revenge.
Still, the young men watch. Their judge
reveals the truth. Why so much care?
The aging judge from upstate states her case.
She's no dog. First Bush, then Palin
made her mad. Revenge was sweet,
lecturing the beastly men that roamed
around her house. Those husbands came
and went,
so many she's not sure that any have
a name. But now her touch is done
for she, as all, is growing old. Her daughter waits
for Russian friends, her boys from Kazakhstan.
Oh, Artemis, where are you now?

Domestic Thought

I.

It was much too long
being fine,
happily in place within a clan.

As if clothes made the man
I'd want or want to be.

And who out there
would ever look?

You hardly need to hide.

(The black ants burrow deeper
when it's cold.
Their villages are bleak,
    John,
beneath the soil.)

II.

Last night all dreams were mine.

I asked to dream about the things
for which I cared
(years ago),
the last oak in the woods,
the largest in the state.

And then I dreamed of you.

Should I, or you, desire
what we'll never be?

I desire being as you become.

III.

If you can keep afloat
until they push us under once again,
hold your breath long enough
not to drown.

IV.

But even when I'd pass another trial,
I'd slip away
in thought.

I'd look for you.

I'd make exceptions.
Wouldn't you?

I never knew
why you,
like all the rest,
were holding back.

Pride

John Climacus in *The Ladder of Divine Ascent* says that doing what one is expected to do and doing it well can make one vain, self-proud, and this, he says, must be repressed, destroyed, in our struggle for purity. Absalom had read this, yet there is such great pleasure in obedience, as we all know, that he could not let go. Obedience, he thought, was what he deeply was; Climacus had been wrong.

Absalom adopted clothing he saw a gay man wear, tho he told himself he was no queer, and he wore these clothes proudly in the privacy of his rooms amidst the studios. His mother had enforced obedience on him from his earliest days, telling him how to act and what to wear, and in the silence of his rooms when she was asleep, he could follow his pleasures to their extreme. He could imagine as he wished, and he wished to imagine the grandest of all joys, the one that comes only when we fully submit to ourselves.

His mother had never treated him in any way in public that the public itself would fault. She was simply what the guidance counselors in his schools called "overly concerned," and that was not unusual for a single mother with responsibilities, they thought. Absalom naturally had a timid nature, was unsure of himself, and, like his mother, seemed deeply religious, which always drives one deeper into thought. The counselors doubted that unless he changed greatly he would ever have a companion in life, his mother excepted, and time proved them right.

What they could not see was how Absalom could construct a private life. That was only for him to know, but it was also where his essence could be found. In one sense he had only a private life as he was no joiner, belonged to no clubs, and spent his spare hours playing video games and surfing the net. When he was twelve, his mother put filters on his computer to keep him from seeing things she did not want him to know, but every boy learns quickly how to evade technical things, and Absalom did and entered sites that fed sexual fantasies that his mother knew only by rumor. As he grew older, these fantasies became each night the entirety of his solitary mind.

He learned that there was a vast fantasy world in which objects played the roles that people did in other lives. He understood the psychological mechanism of sexuality better than those who say that they "fall in love." Most men and women, he knew, project their innerness onto other beings, whom they never really know or want to know, and so wake up one morning, after many years of marriage, wondering who that being sleeping beside them really is.

On the web, Absalom found a universe of solitaries like himself, women and men who had chosen objects such as articles of clothing and sexual toys to serve functions that another person conventionally would. Further, it was claimed, the results were far more intense than the merely human could provide. Absalom studied this way of living, fascinated by the varieties possible in his sensual universe and chose for himself one of its most florid, if decadent, gardens and cultivated it.

There was a young gay artist who rented one of the studios and who rode a motorcycle, a Supersport, which he parked within view of Absalom's bedroom window. The bike fascinated Absalom, thrilled him, not as something he himself might ride, but as an emblem of what he kept private, for is it not privacy that motorcycles most clearly bespeak?

More than the motorcycle, the leather jacket and pants the artist wore delighted Absalom. They were black with blue and red stripes and fit their owner perfectly and had chains attached.

Unknown to his mother, Absalom searched the web until he found leathers and chains identical to those the artist wore. Absalom purchased them and took pleasure dressing in them in private. While other men might lie next to their beloveds and smooth his or her skin, he would lie on his bed in his costume, sliding his hands back and forth, and imagine he was riding in the Rockies or the Alps, neither of which he had actually seen nor wished to see, for what mattered was not that they existed but that he could imagine that they did, and thereby enter a fluid fantasy which itself now took charge of all things, even his breath.

He would run his hands along his leather pants and caress the jacket and the chains suspended from it in the same way that a husband might caress his wife. He could imagine himself in his gear riding fast along a cliff, endangering himself, hitting an oil spill perhaps or a stretch of sand, losing control of everything, and flying out over the edge. He could then submit fully, for there is no greater submission than when we know we are about to die.

What happened now felt as things should when left to pursue their natural ends: cutting through empty space, losing all control.

Thus Absalom overcame and released himself. Pain and fear dissolved in a breath that those who would take their pleasure in others can never know. He had reached the ecstacy of pride, its highest form, in which things become vehicles that reveal themselves as what we most intensely are.

Midas in Istanbul

"And thus [the beloved] . . . loves, but he knows not what; he does not understand and cannot explain his own state; he appears to have caught the infection of blindness from another; the lover is his mirror in whom he is beholding himself, but he is not aware of this."
—Plato, *Phaedrus,* trans. Benjamin Jowett

I captured them. I took them home and taught them how to please me by their dress. Each was made to wear the fashions one season singled out as style. No two could wear the same. I took them to my yacht and sailed around the bay. I took their photos, and I lay with those I liked. We watched the sun come up and drank a toast to style. They honored me with wishes for a long and happy life: "To what we see!" they said. I took them back to bars and clubs and watched them dance the night away.

They were my friends, my only friends. There are so few that any of us trust, but these were earnest and did the things I asked.

All Aflutter

an admonition for C. and his ways with other men

"He that trusteth his own heart is a fool." —Proverbs, 28:26

Married! The classic fibrillation!
My heart can barely break, dear C.

You feel
the middle class
will save our day.

Wait! Not so fast!

No single therapy is good
for one and all.

It's fair to say:

Never use another man
for private ends
unless fate leads your way.

The answer to your self-regard
is etched on glass:

Dear C.:
Keep your condo clean,
your garden free of weeds.

The time will come
when being nice
won't be enough.

ÇORUM SAMSUN BAFRA
İZMİR ANKARA E.ŞEHİR
MERAM
KONYA-ADANA
AYDIN
TURİZM
MARMARIS BODRUM
TRABZON
KÖSEOĞLU
DENİZLİ-NAZİLLİ-AYDIN
SÖKE-DİDİM-KUŞADASI

Lust

Everything seen from the doorway, from the window, from the entrance to another room. Everything seen is possessed. We collect these images as we collect our feelings and find they are the same; we do not need to touch.

Our minds are albums of desire and what we don't desire. The albums are what we are. Augustine told us that the great thing was to love, and love is compassion, which is much too easy, cheap. That toward which we feel compassion is what we also are. We save compassion for our work and family festivals and other things that matter less than what desire makes its own. There is nothing worthy but our mental albums, in the end.

I've arranged mine with tremendous care. Here in this village of things (the seeds that have made me what I am), this village is a place where everything looks old but has a vibrancy you can't imagine (it must clasp you; it must be fuel that gives your winter warmth). I collect my images on streets and in the malls. In churches. In my office among my patients. On my travels. I can claim to be no more than things I see. That's all we are.

A few small images I capture with my camera, to hold them still, and frame them for my office wall. I've surfed the net in search of more.

We've heard Mormon missionaries say they want the names of everyone who's lived. The names are kept in vaults for just their church and God to see. Imagine names as pictures, our pleasant horde of images in vaults, broken open only when we service what they need, and with ferocious speed we feel their essence as the moment breaks us from within. Inside these beings that our images create, we lave ourselves and enter joy and hold ourselves transfixed by night.

To my patients, photos on my office walls seem only documents of places I have been, yet I treasure these images in other ways and brush my hands like fleece across their surfaces.

Years ago I walked along a beach near Alexandria and thought of Callimachus and the way he loved. I saw two youths embrace beside a dune and knew exactly why Apollo's seen only by the good and why youth must not be still when he visits there. I saw Cavafy's grave and realized he'd felt the way I do. I saw the spot where Alexander lay for centuries, and in my mind all this added up to more than what you read, more than just the words. You know such final truths only when you deeply know yourself.

I swam in reed lagoons and closed my eyes to old rich houses near the shore. I wanted just the feel of wet reeds on my chest.

We are given so few years, I tell my patients, and as they wish, I prescribe their medications just as the god Asclepias once did. But all this comes to nothing when my work is done, my secretary's gone, and I can close the door. The money's earned; the patients' bodies work. I've given, all day long, medicines that make my patients feel the way they think they should.

Then the work of living starts again or should, theirs as well as mine, and there's nothing in it worth those medications or the mounds of goods in stores, buying/selling things, for they can give us nothing that our god Apollo can. All that matters is that I see everything I can and store the good parts in my albums, ready for release. That release is my Pandora's jar, sweet smelling, pouring out dark fluid joy that only ends when morning makes me work again.

I know my patients well and hear them worry over things they cannot change. I've known many men who only want to please their wives and, fearful, ask me for the pills so as to be the men they think they need to be. Such silly men they are: my friends, these men are fifty, sixty, even more, and it's time for them to stop performing as if making love were something that must be seen. There's a better world for older men. There always was.

Their beings, flaccid skin, have cracked apart and become aging, incoherent needs to reproduce what once was intimately felt. I used to think that just my women patients were the ones who suffered from a need to see themselves displayed in love but now it seems the universal creed, and I find these aging men insisting that they have to please in order that they please themselves.

But as for me, I think again of copper-colored gods who burned the sand for me in Egypt, the boys beside that dune. What pathos, given scenes like that, must we all feel for those encapsulated in the rooms they know too well where just some old performance is enforced.

I stand here in my solitary space and have no wish. My patients have their pleasures as they want. The world moves on. The traffic doesn't stop. As for me, I only need to walk toward that bright dune, for that's enough, far more than those sad husbands ever know.

The Politics of One

"sic amet ipse licet, sic non potiatur amato!"
—Ovid, Metamorphosis

[*Narcissus was the beautiful boy with whom it was easy to fall in love, but he rejected all comers until one, seeking vengeance for having been slighted, cursed him by asking that he himself love in vain and thereby know how it is to have one's desires denied. Nemesis heard, and the curse was set, but the consequences were not what the rejected lover had supposed. By falling in love with himself, Narcissus achieved the highest love, in which one's entirety meets and fulfills itself. There are no boundaries; there is no other; yet there is response, for everything Narcissus does, the reflection does as well. Obedience, submission are entire, but there is no struggle, and nothing remains after the finalities of completion but lassitude and surfeit.*]

Admonitions weren't enough for you.
You were too stylish, clothed, too proper,
too medieval in your operatic domicile,
all that decoration as if set design
could make a home, releasing
nothing that you'd have alone.

Dear Crazy J., the sun you saw has no horizon.
The light that made boys alter all you know,
a twisted ribbon with which your gentle,
sweet, abandoned self will mark
no more than chapters in the book
you write to read yourself.

Hidden in your cabinet
you keep your shehrengiz,
details in verse about the local boys,
workers at the dock, tin-smiths, pedlars,
the brave who kept their dancing bears at home,

such that, whomever you might see,
you'll find to be no more than just yourself:
your wish, your need, your flinching eyes,
incandescent in a moral dare,
wary, beneficent, but rarely kind.

You play the gentle priest,
radiate a midnight dance,
say you're mine,
but pause, consult your frame,
pretend your fate is wrapped
in other hands.

So reasoned, all thought out,
every movement done
in line with common thought,
so that you never reach
the boy you think to touch.

"Quod cupio, mecum est,"
the lover, pleading, said:
"inopem me copia fecit."

A Lean and Hungry Look

They say I think too much,
but if that fellow won't look back, or can't
(his training being much as mine once was),
who's left to correspond? — To correspond:
to be the same or opposite,
the perfect match.

That was what we wished for way back when.
Today the images collide,
their colors break out from forms and make
my spectral skies of ecstasy, which is to say
the ones collected in my mind can't bed with just any you,
and yet they formulate a new extreme where passion
occupies a fractal universe, wholly mine.

The ones I'd love are gone; their children's
children serve me in the market, bring coffee
to my table when I ask and pay. They leave at night
for rooms I never see. What makes them,
all together in my mind, more than what their fathers were?

Is this the route all follow, or was it meant
as mine? Here ambition takes the face of care,
repeats where I have been. The beach defines itself.
There I find the hands imagination holds
in my wizened mind. I'm old.

And so I would be ready, John.
No expectations,
yet my good will holds me back. I must
depend on pictures. Let's
sit beside salt water, gesticulate.

I like the one displayed beside us.
He's thinking he's the first to feel
the way he does.

He hasn't seen the other soldiers yet;
he doesn't know that he's alone. I'm wanting
just his features as a memory before he's
in the trenches, before he loses life.
Touching in the mind is worthier than life.

My inner village is a set of images, perfections.
My gaze is self-produced. Fashion made
him wear that tight white bathing suit, not
knowing what I'd see in him. He's my display
and comes for free.

His limbs, resilient, submit to sleep.
I have so much. Privacy is nothing to
the mind. He cannot hesitate unless
I want him to. He will never understand.
He will never see.

He'll never run from this bare room
that I define, in which my wizard self
can work its will traducing lineaments
to make that body feel less worthy
and, now humbled, look the way it should.

The old men gather on the boardwalk
as if a dream of wife were all there were,
some lady lost in games played long ago,
but here beside the water all is new.
The beach defines itself.

Ecstatic isolation is the only fact
my ending will allow.

Notes

Epigraphs:

Samuel Hopkins: Eighteenth-century thinkers such as David Hume believed that self-interest ultimately serves the public good. Jonathan Edwards disagreed, arguing in *The Nature of True Virtue* (1865) that "[s]elf-love is by nobody mistaken for true virtue." Samuel Hopkins, Edwards's student, pushed the argument further, concluding, "All sin consists in self-love and what is implied in this." Although less well known than the others cited here, Hopkins was critical to the early formation of an American sensibility, at least until the mid-nineteenth century found his theology overly reasoned — e.g., Oliver Wendell Holmes's "The Deacon's Masterpiece" (1858).

"A Problem with Poems"

"*Ut pictura poesis.*": "As is painting, so is poetry."

"His Sons Grow Old":

Sultan Murad III: died 1595. The boy's murder was accomplished on the orders of Murat's son and successor, Mehmed III.

"Pride":

John Climacus: sixth-century monk, whose *The Ladder of Divine Ascent* describes the process through which one may achieve oneness with God.

"The Politics of One":

"*sic amet ipse licet, sic non potiatur amato!*": the curse that Narcissus love but that the love be unrequited.

shehrengiz: a genre of Ottoman poetry written by older, cultivated men about the beautiful, working-class boys whom they knew in the community.

"Quod cupio, mecum est, / inopem me copia fecit. ": Narcissus's complaint, implying that a surfeit of self-love impoverishes as it enriches.

Echo, however important in Ovid's version, appears to be a late addition to the story, complicating it, but also, it may be, obscuring the earlier emphasis on seeing as the passage that Narcissus follows to achieve his ecstacy. (Cf. James Davidson's comments on the story in *The Greeks and Greek Love* [Random House, 2007], pp. 13-14.)

"A Lean and Hungry Look"

"Yond Cassius has a lean and hungry look,
He thinks too much; such men are dangerous."
 —spoken by Caesar in Shakespeare, *Julius Caesar*